EMOJI WORLD
24 PAGE COLORING BOOK

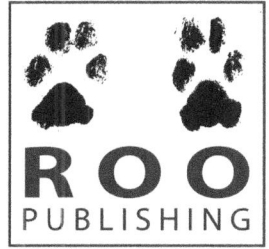

ROO
PUBLISHING

Illustrations by Dani Kates

Dear Colorer,

My name is Dani and I drew the pictures in this coloring book!
I'm an artist, a designer, and a HUGE fan of coloring.
When I buy a coloring book, the first thing I do is take a thin black pen and
draw tiny detailed lines and patterns to make the pictures more fun to color.
I love doing it so much that I decided to design my own coloring books with the
same type of detailed lines and fun patterns.

All of those details and lines make this is an "adult" style coloring book,
but the pictures are way more fun to color!

This one is all about Emojis. They're EVERYWHERE!
On clothes, in the water, up in the sky and even on Pizza!

So have fun, color something amazing and share it with me on social media!

@ColorWithDani
#ColorWithDani

XOXO,
Dani Kates

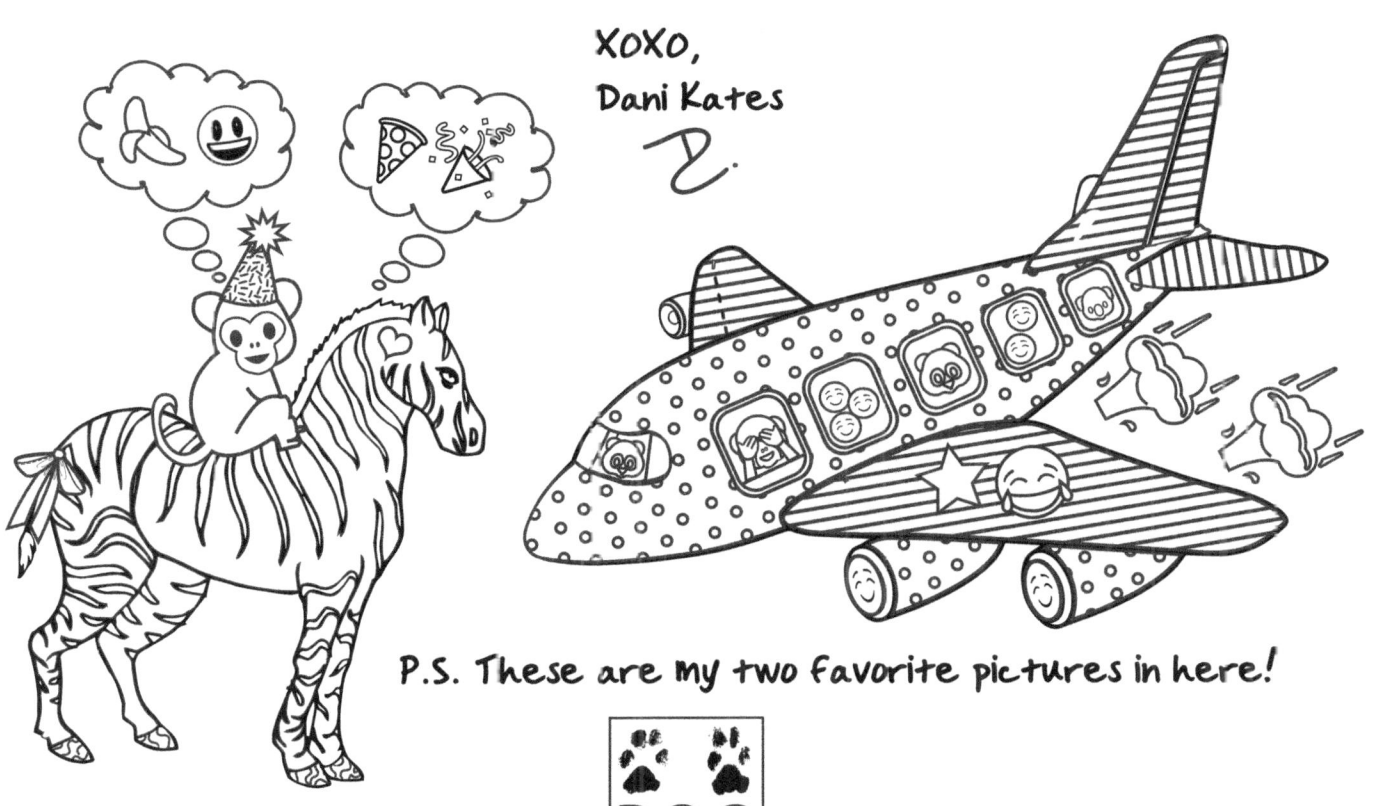

P.S. These are my two favorite pictures in here!

ROO
PUBLISHING

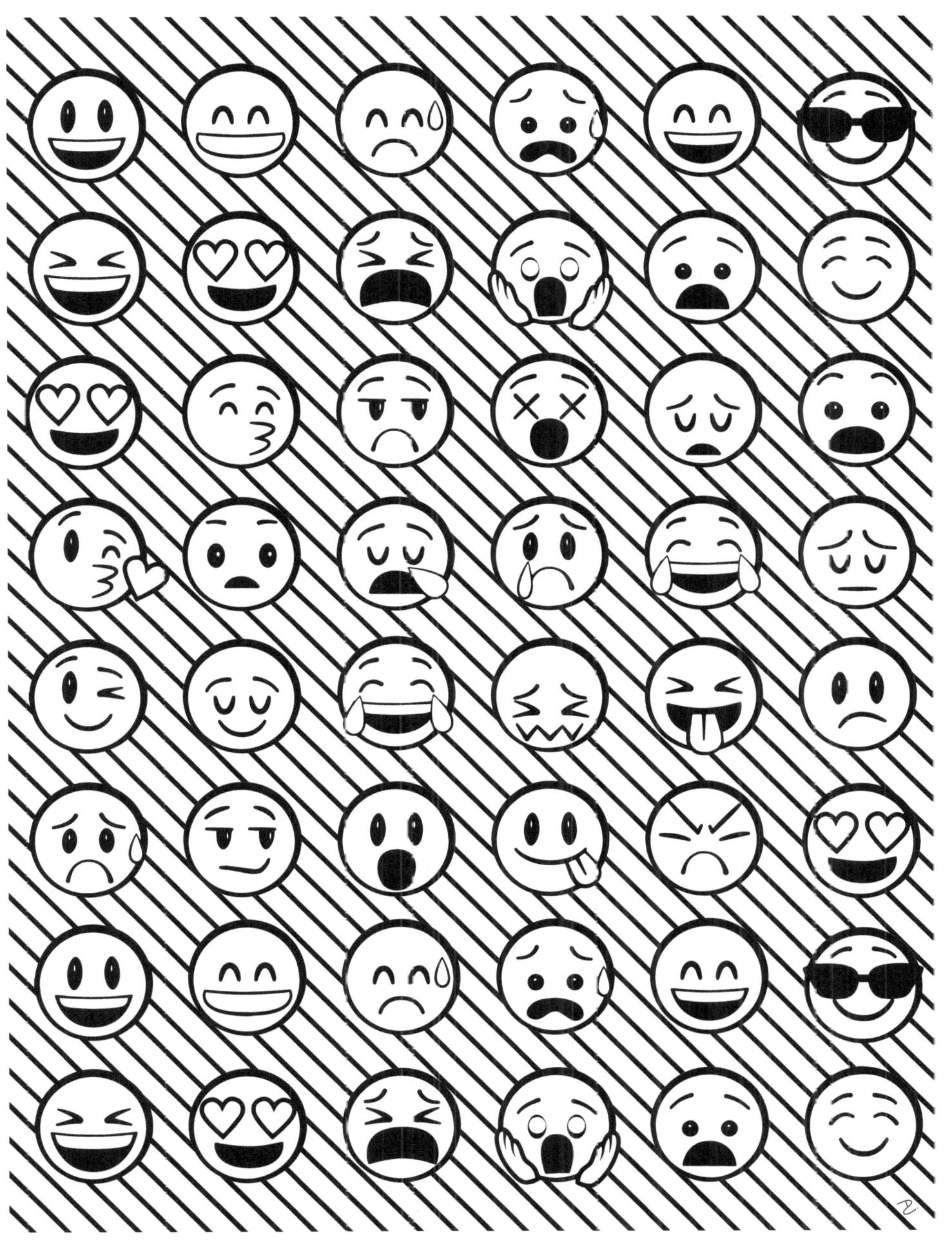

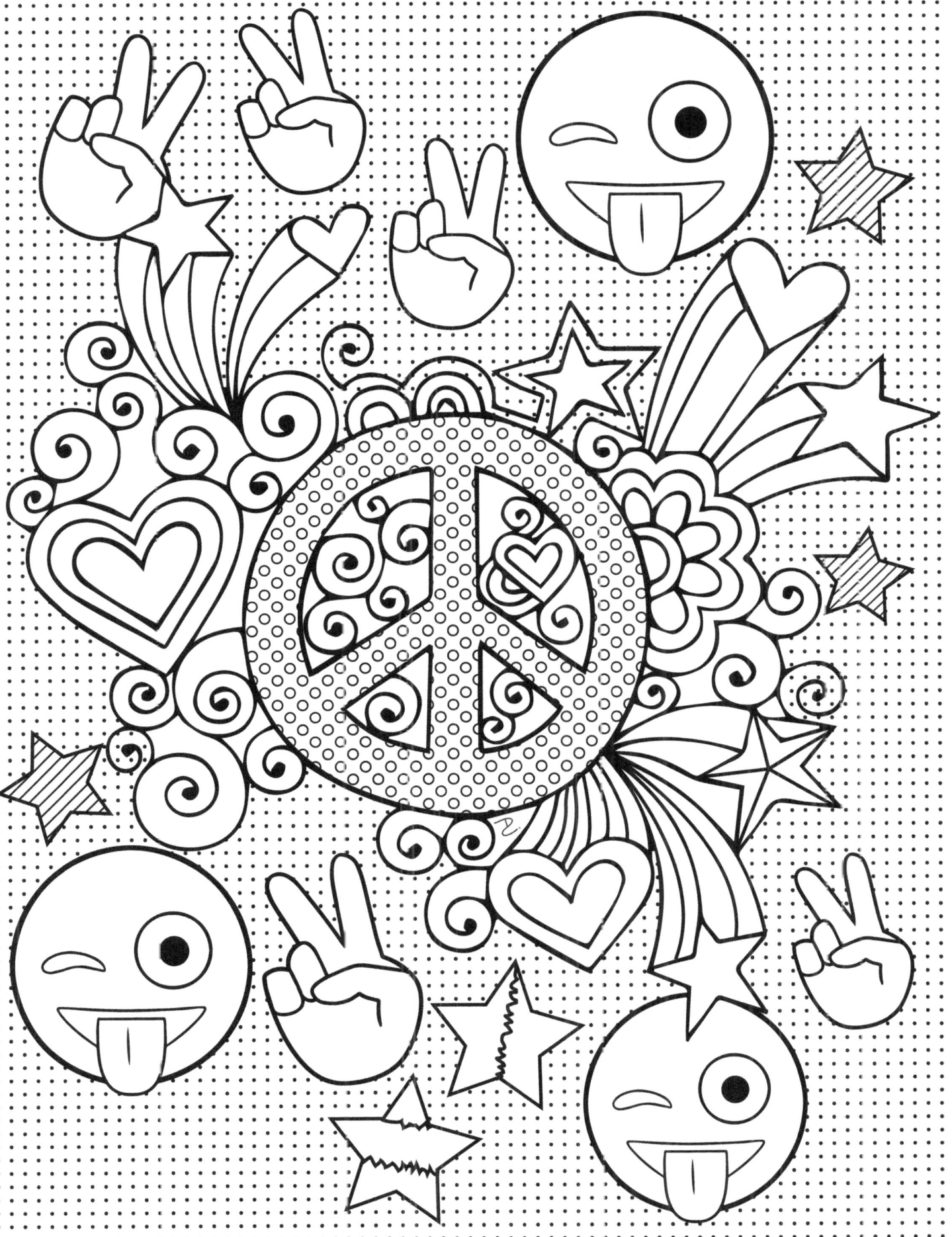

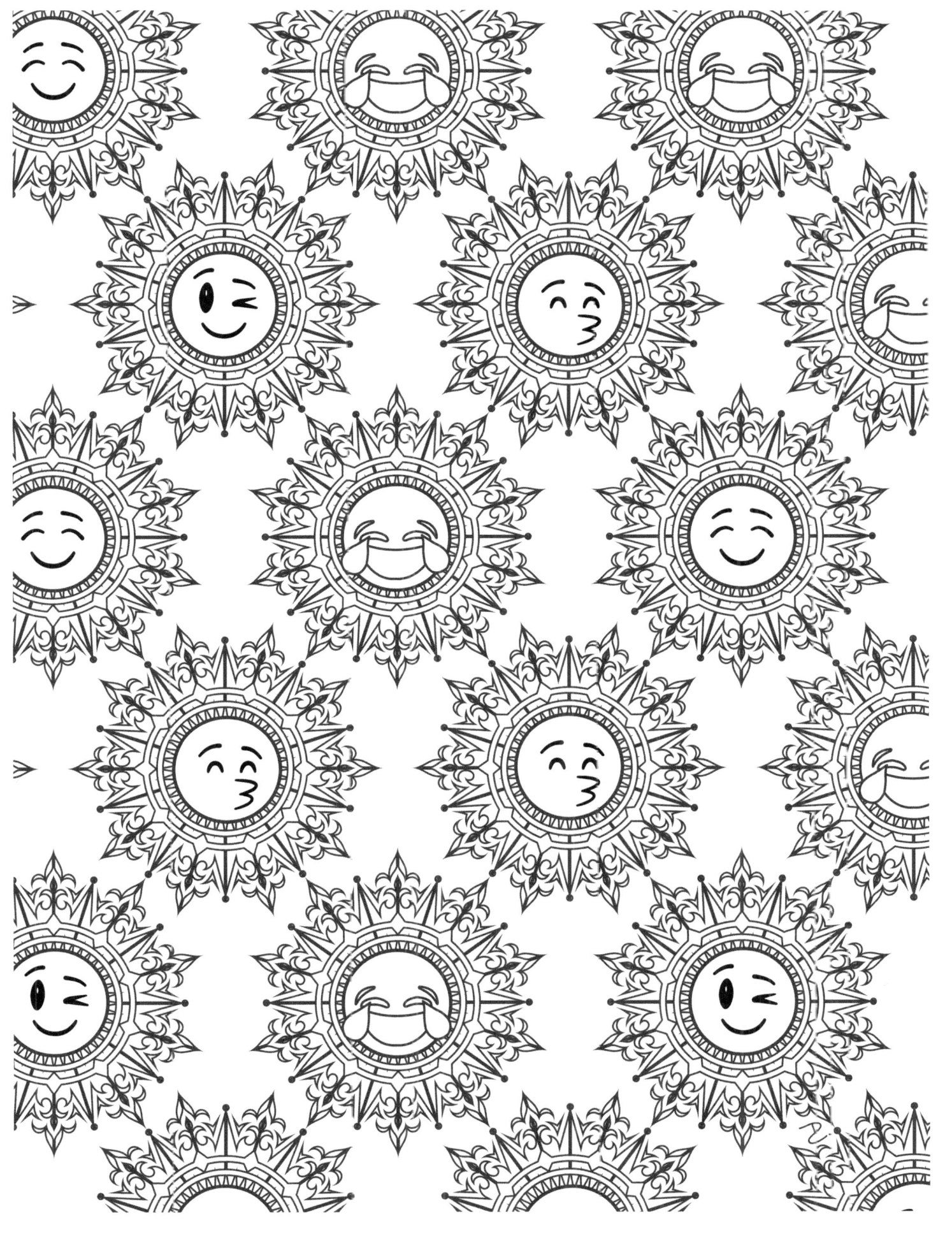

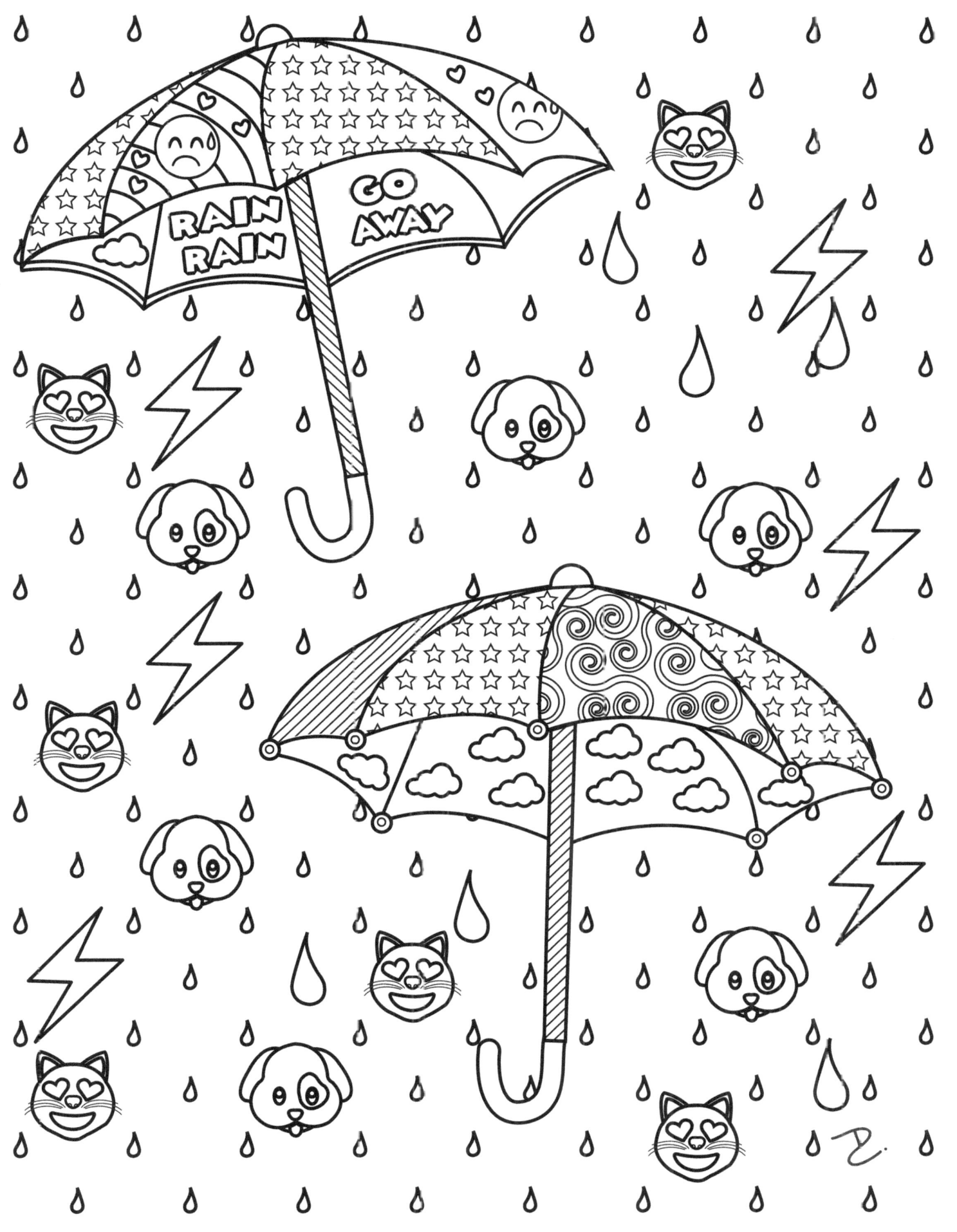

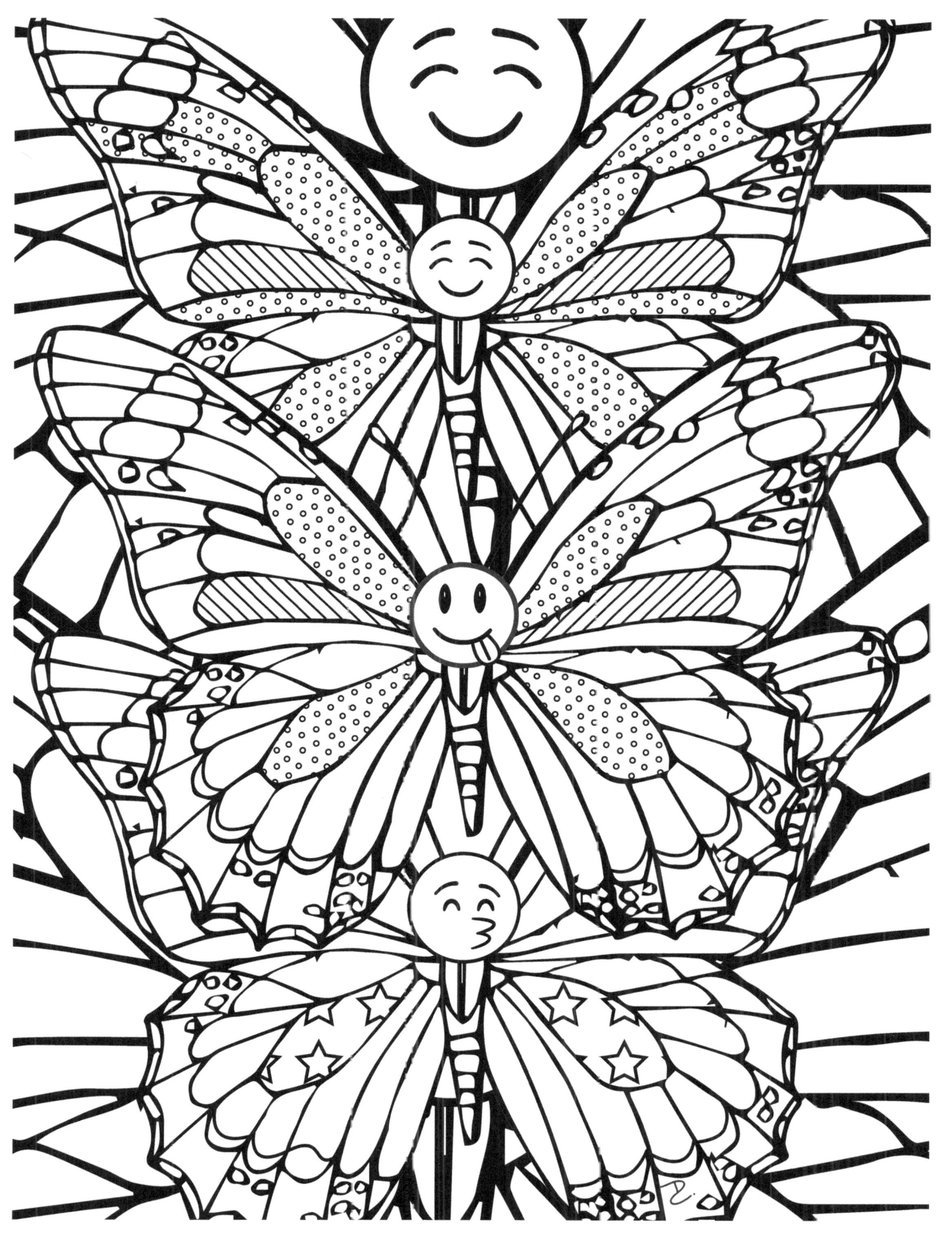

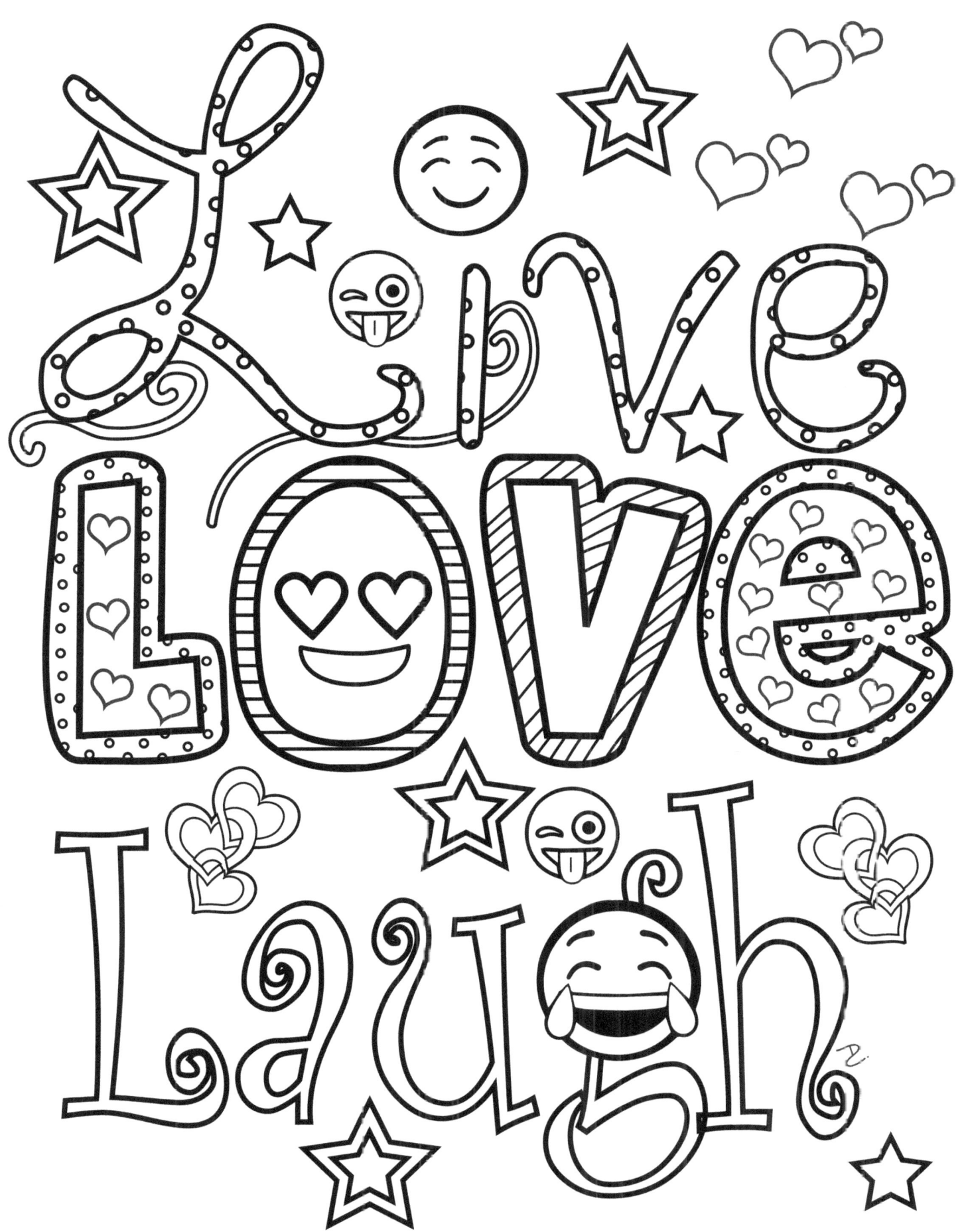

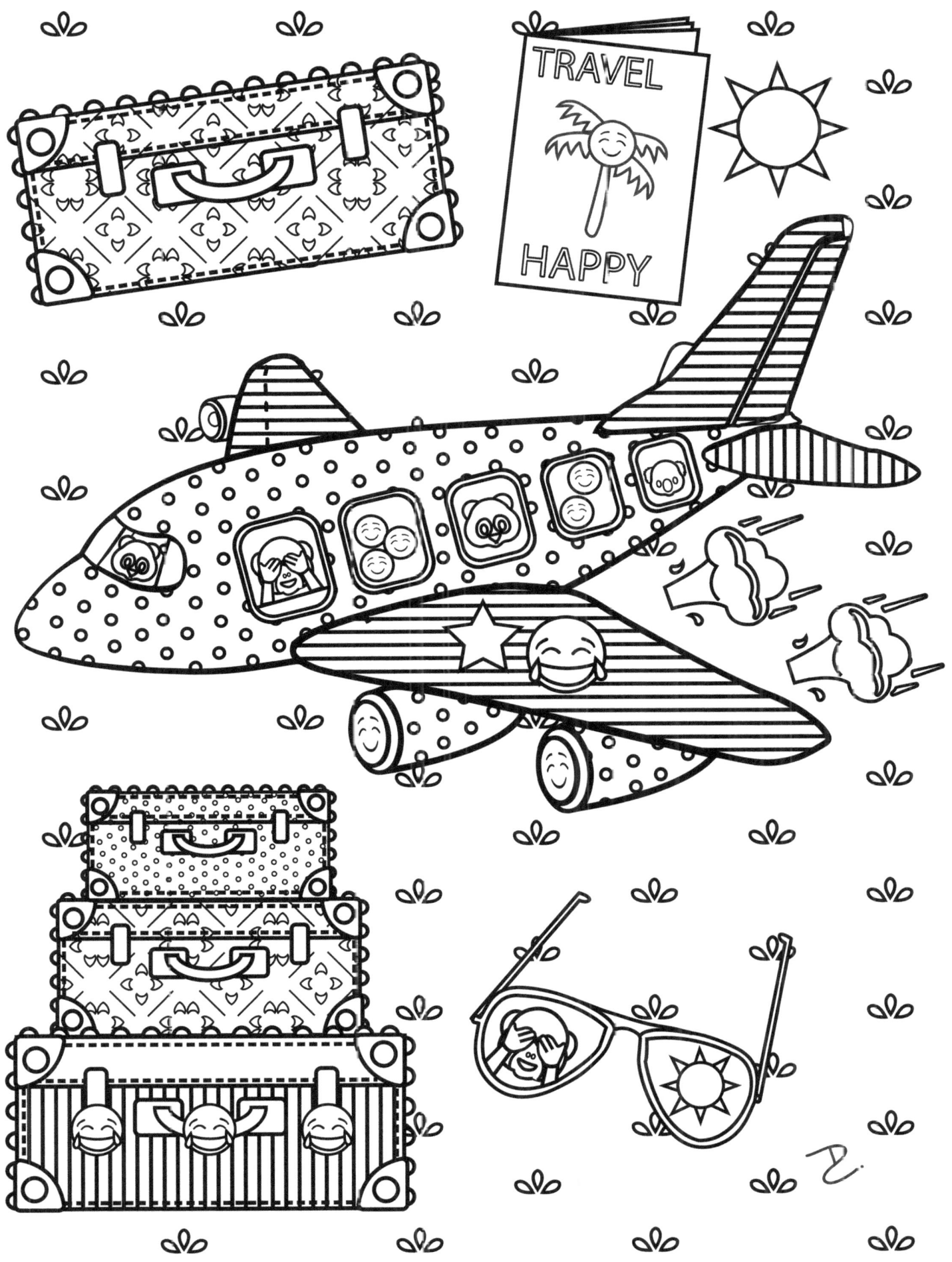

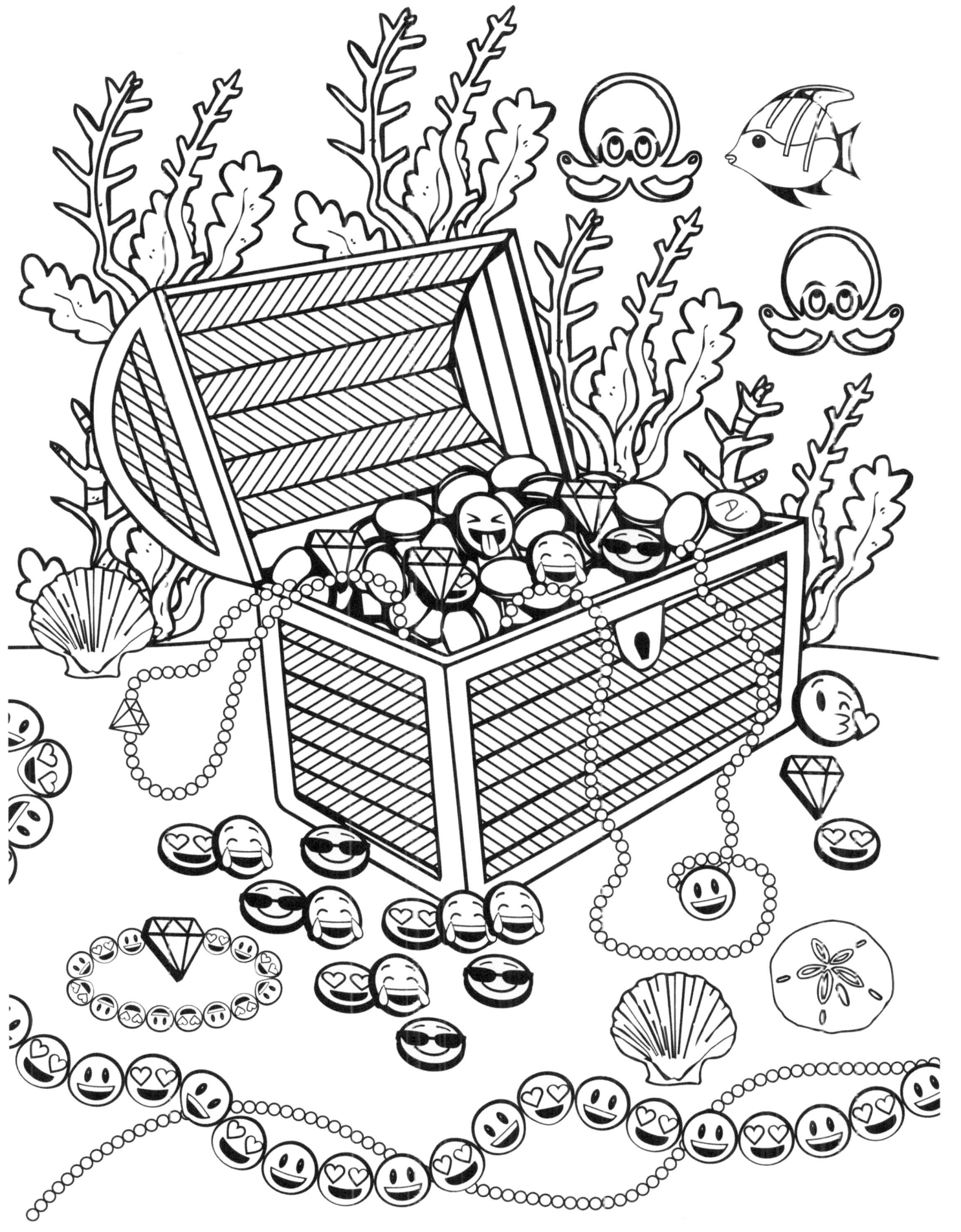

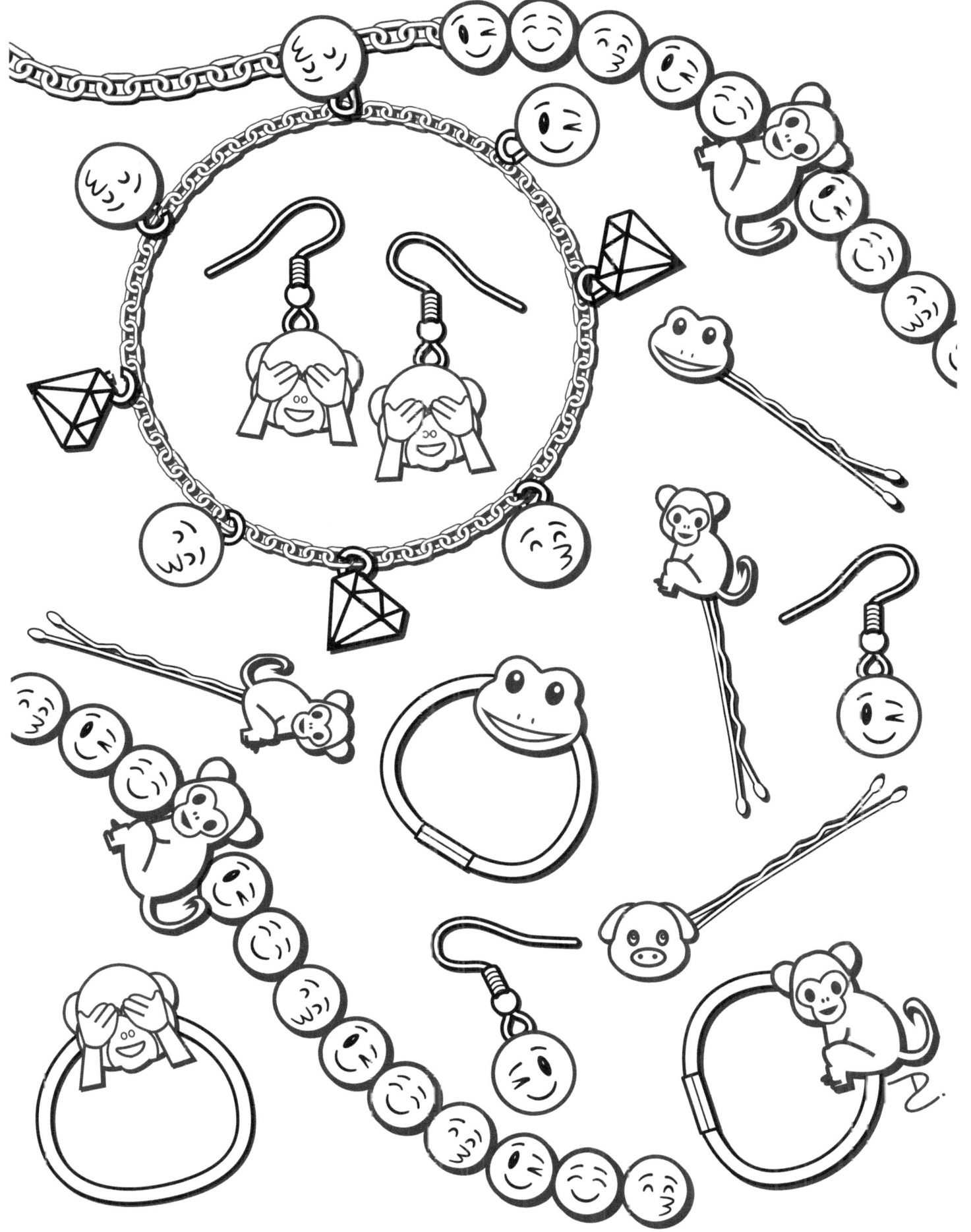

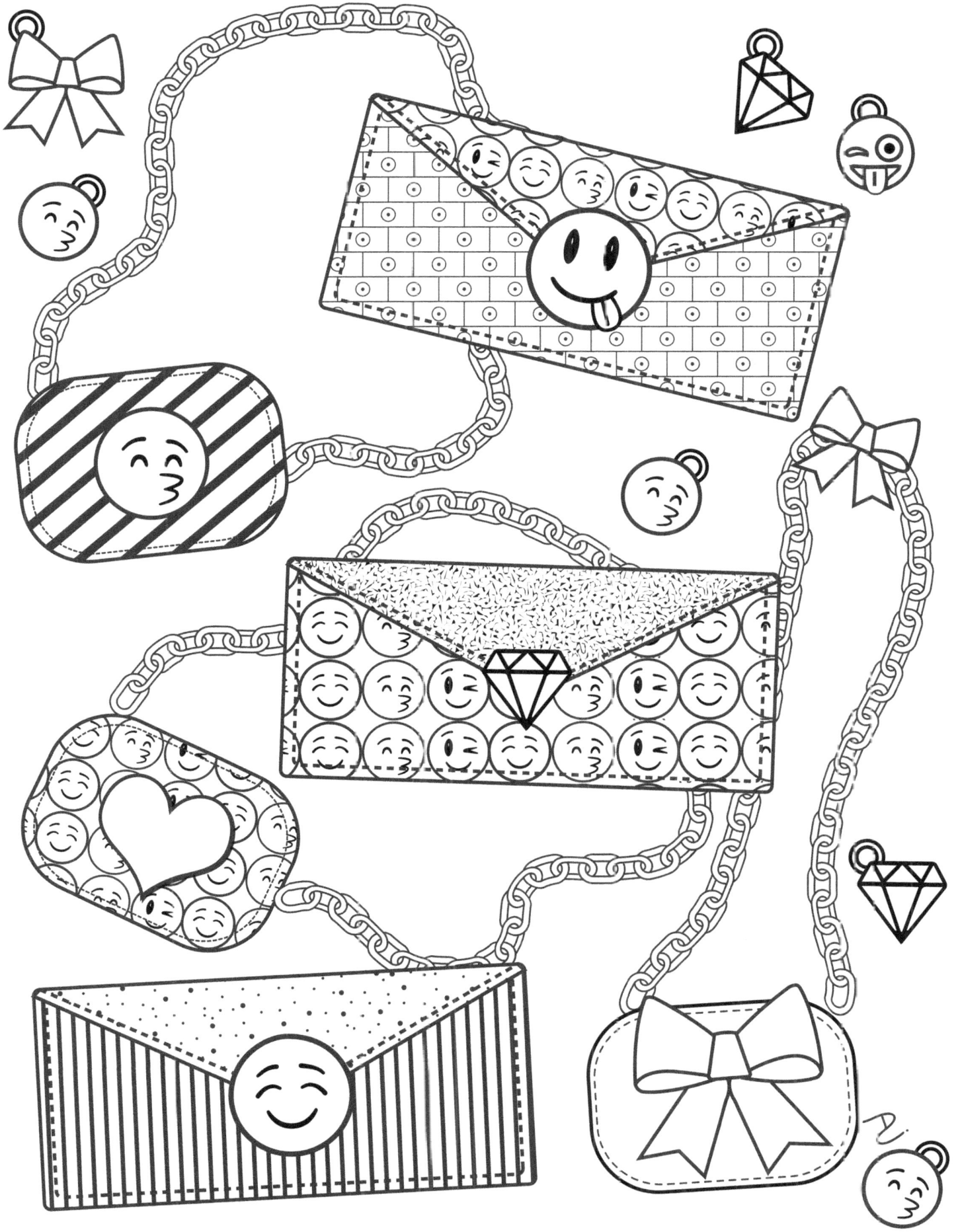

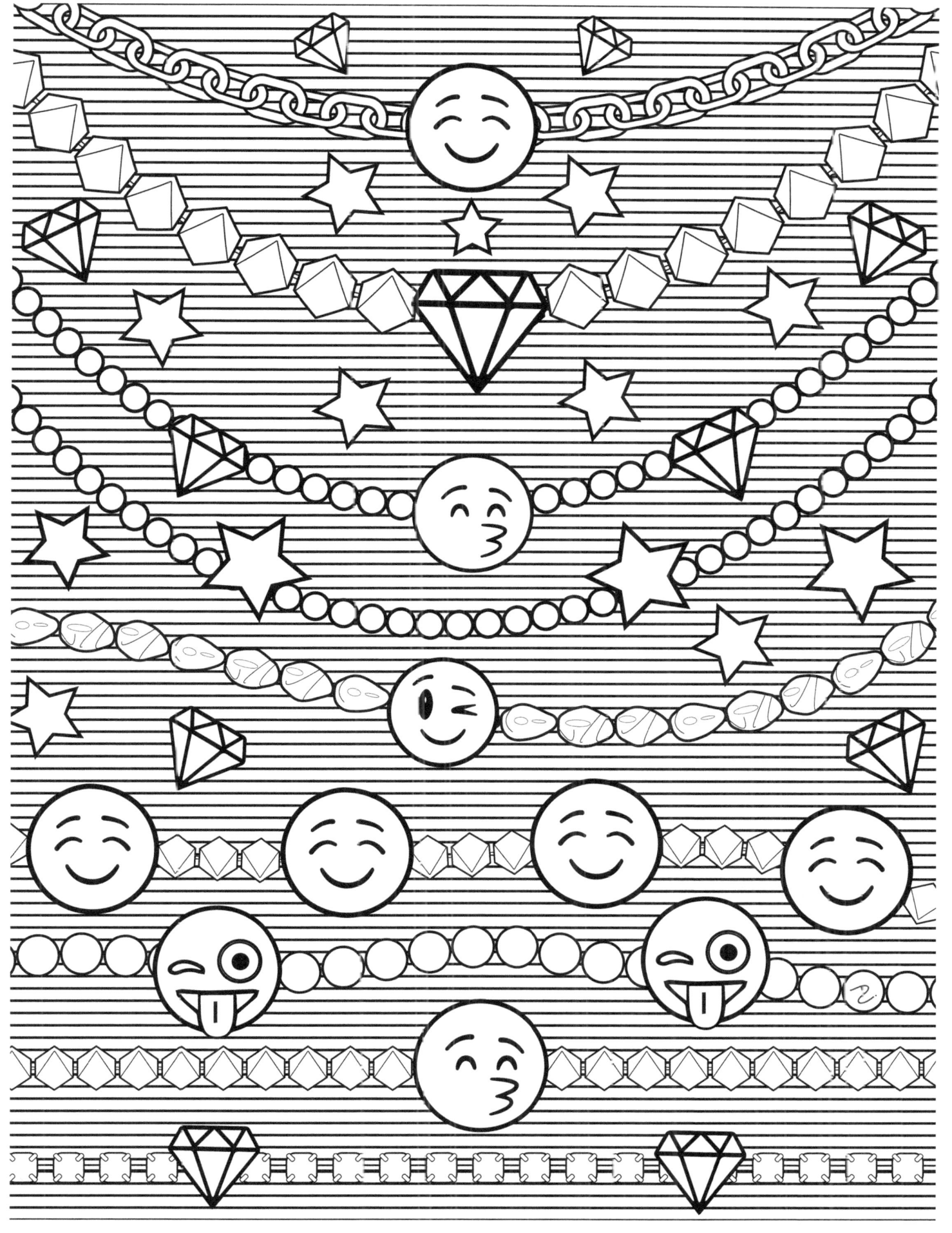

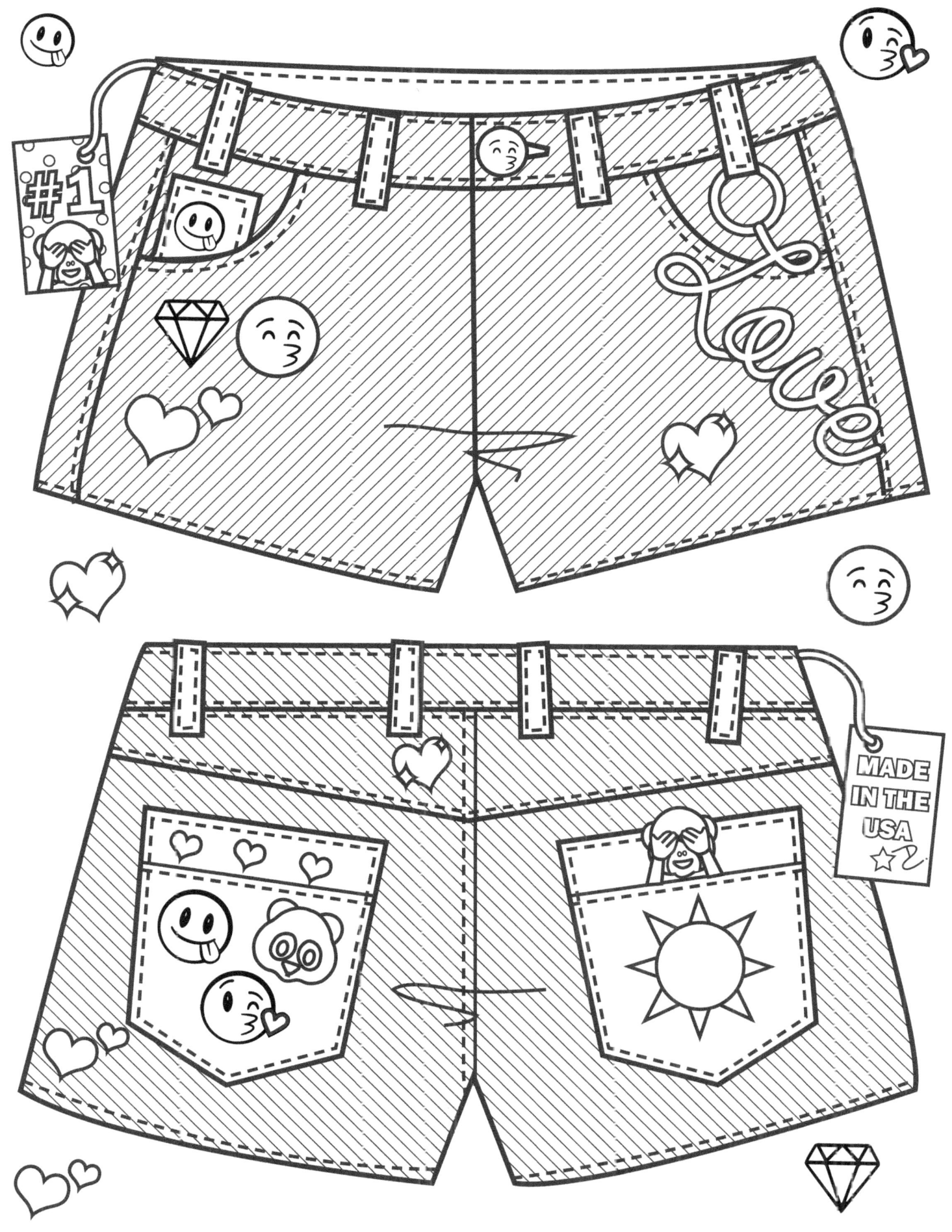

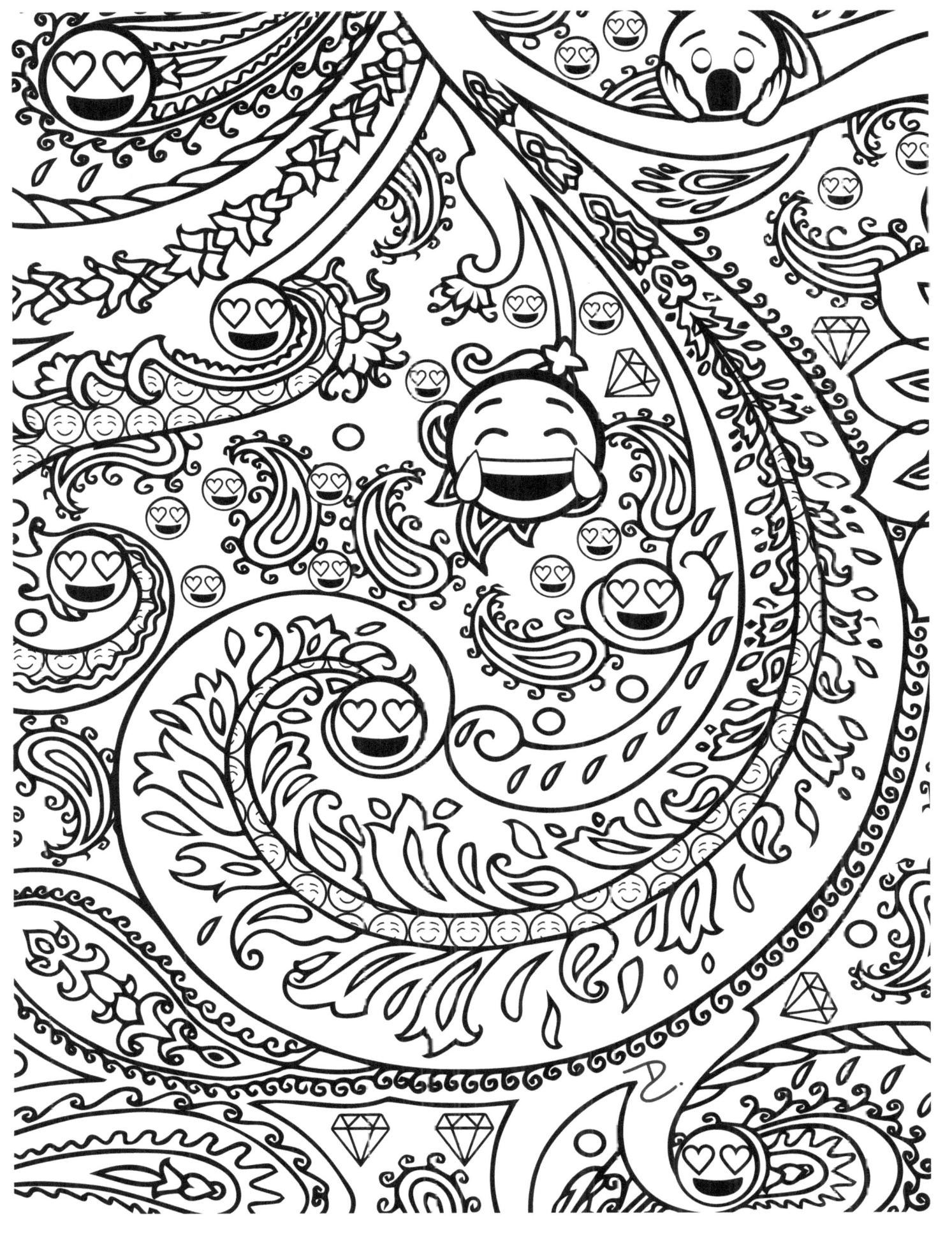

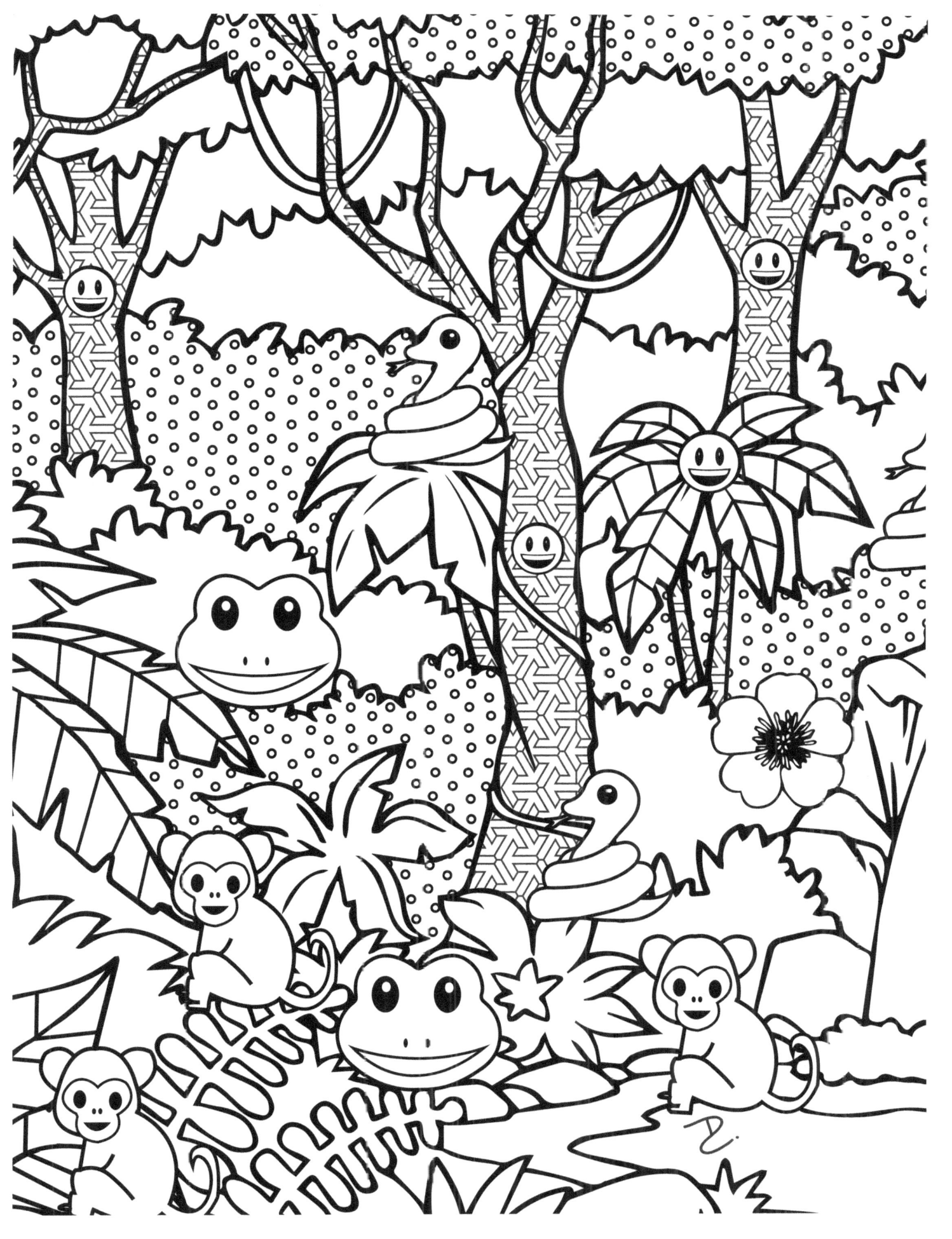

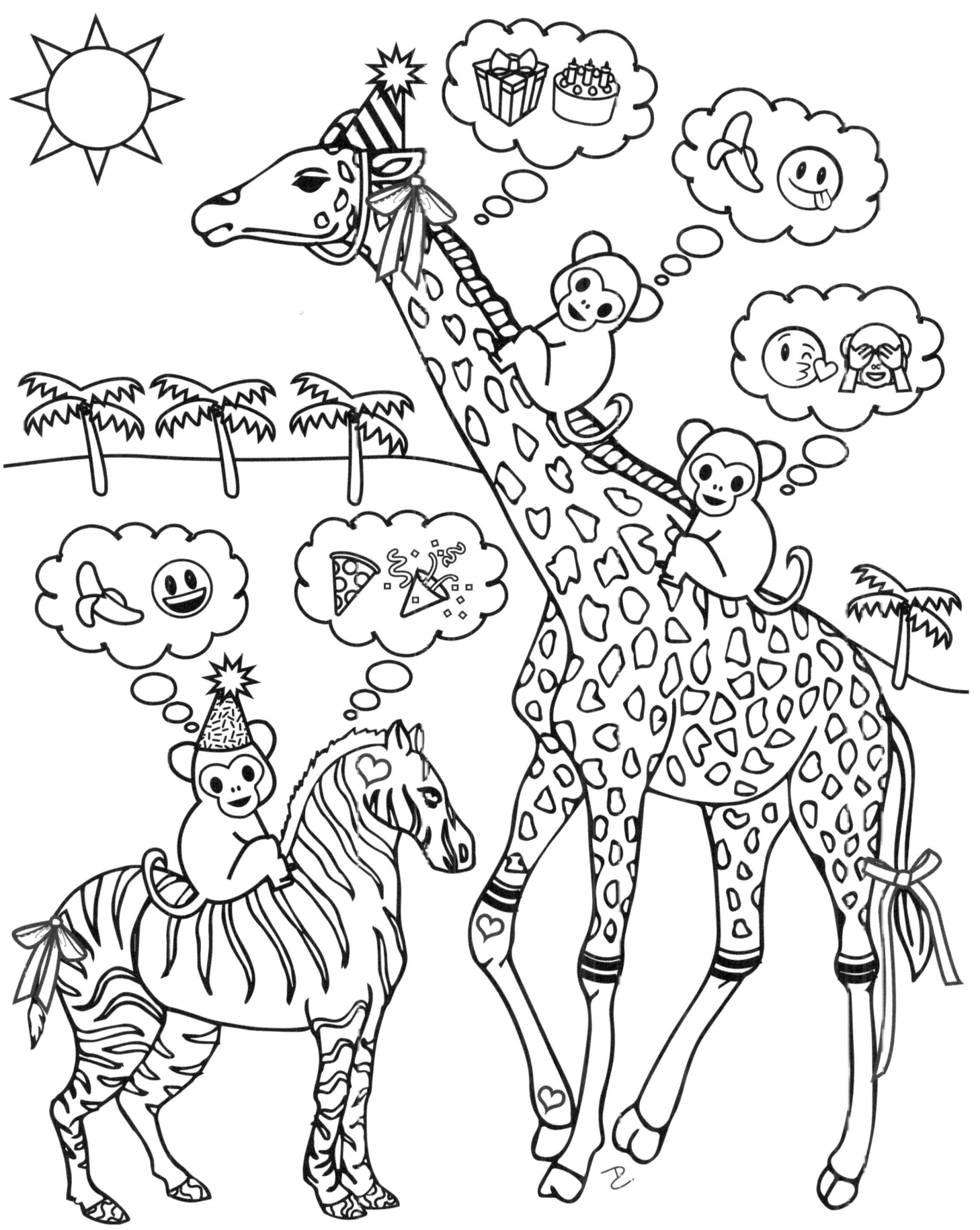

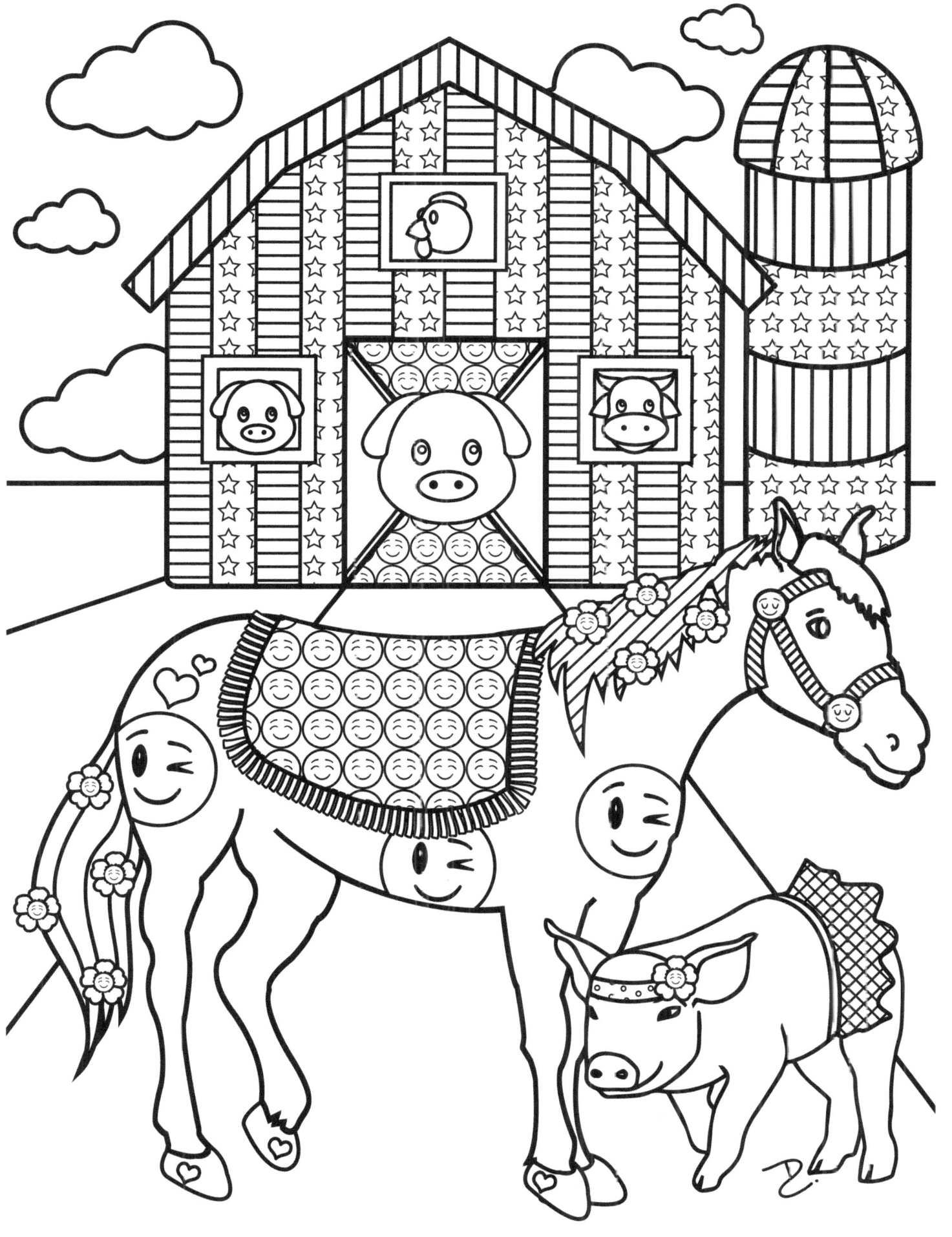

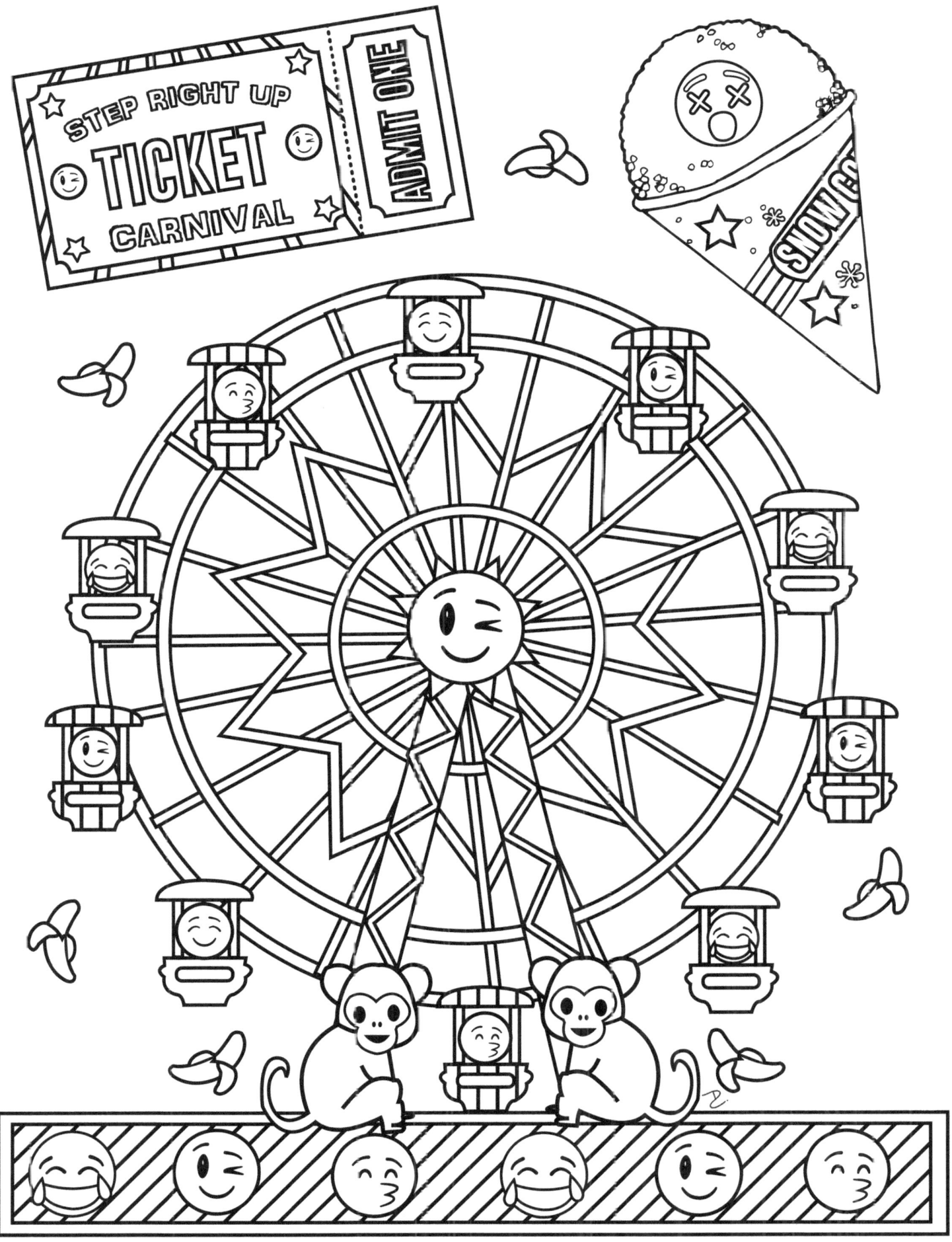

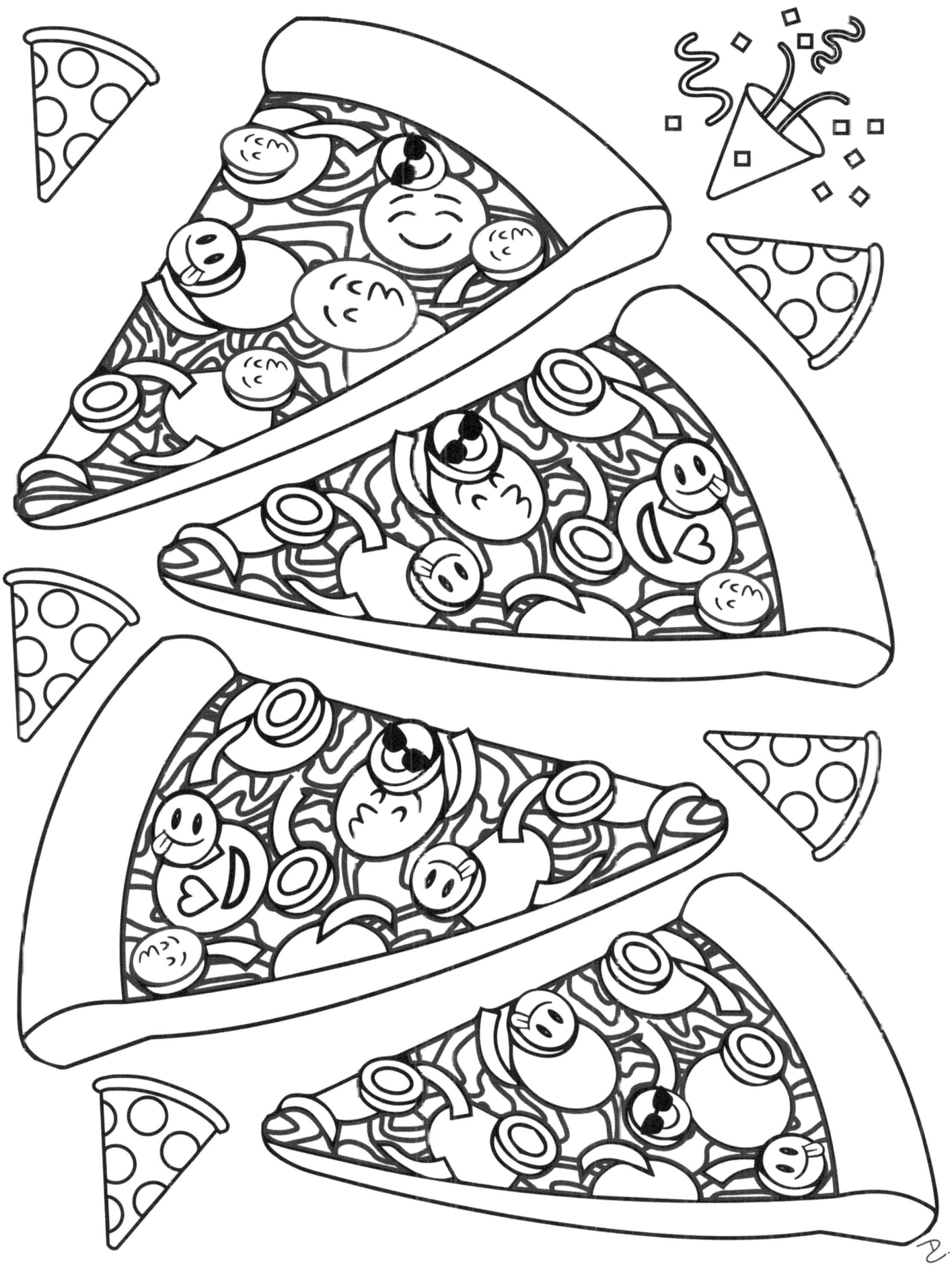

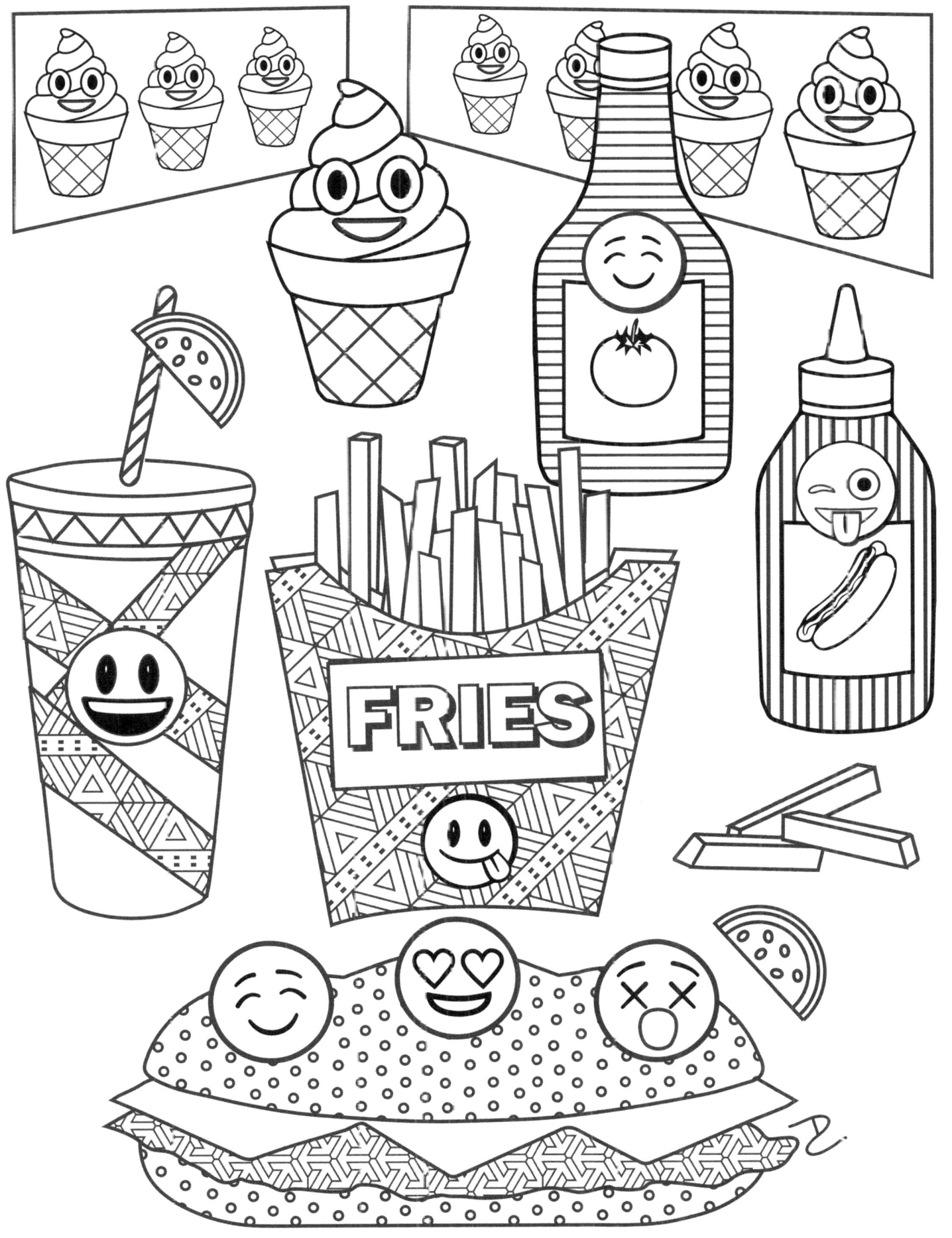

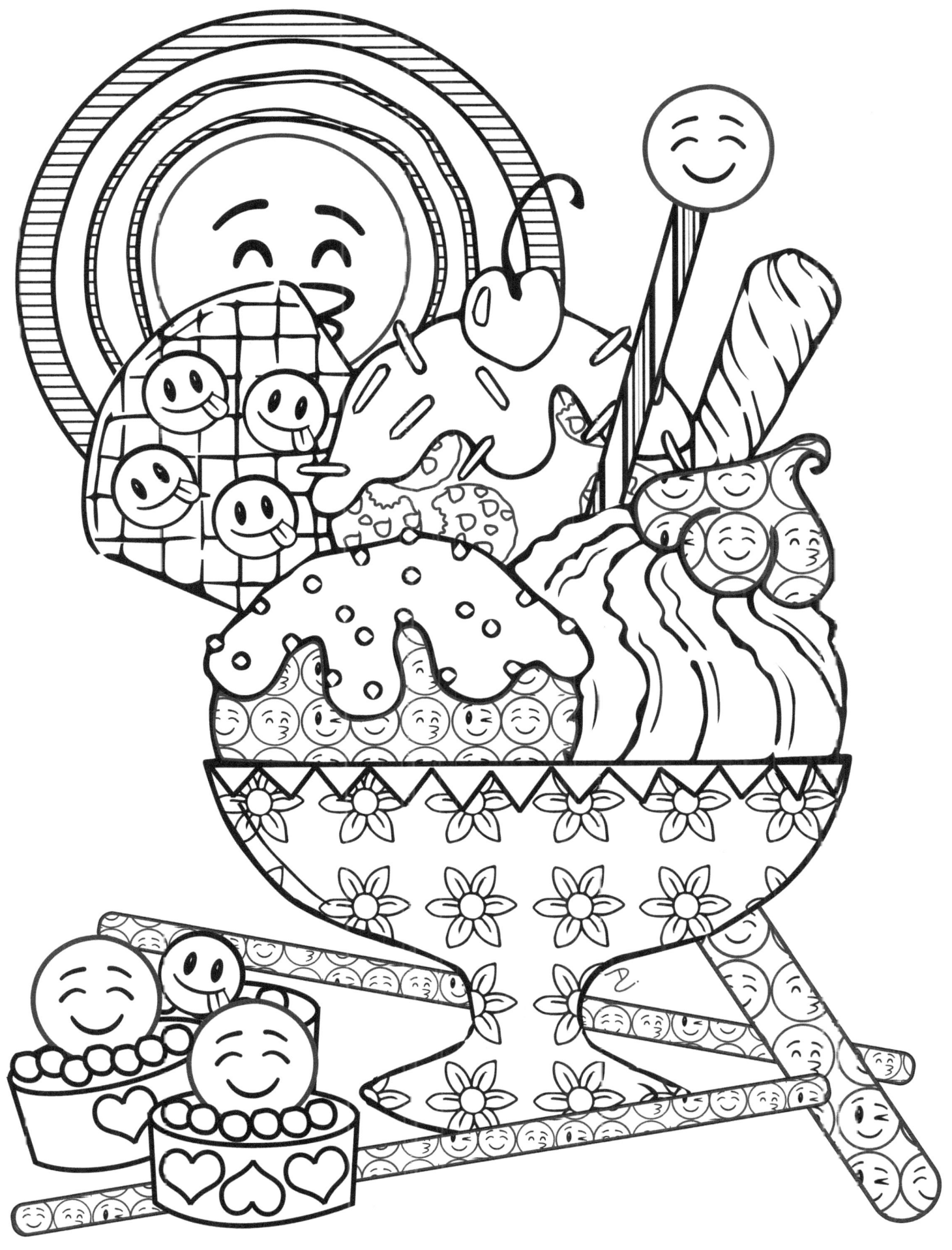

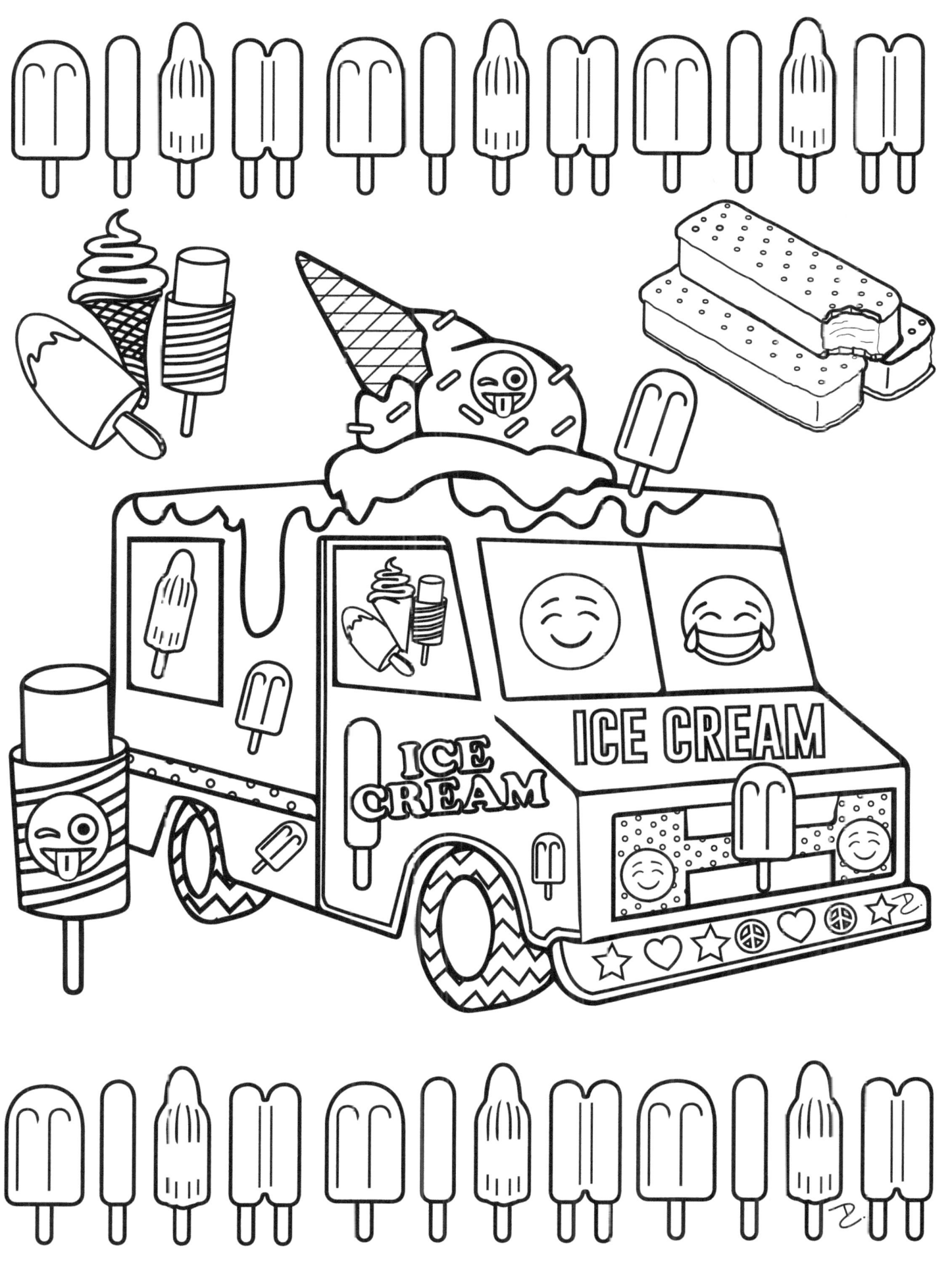

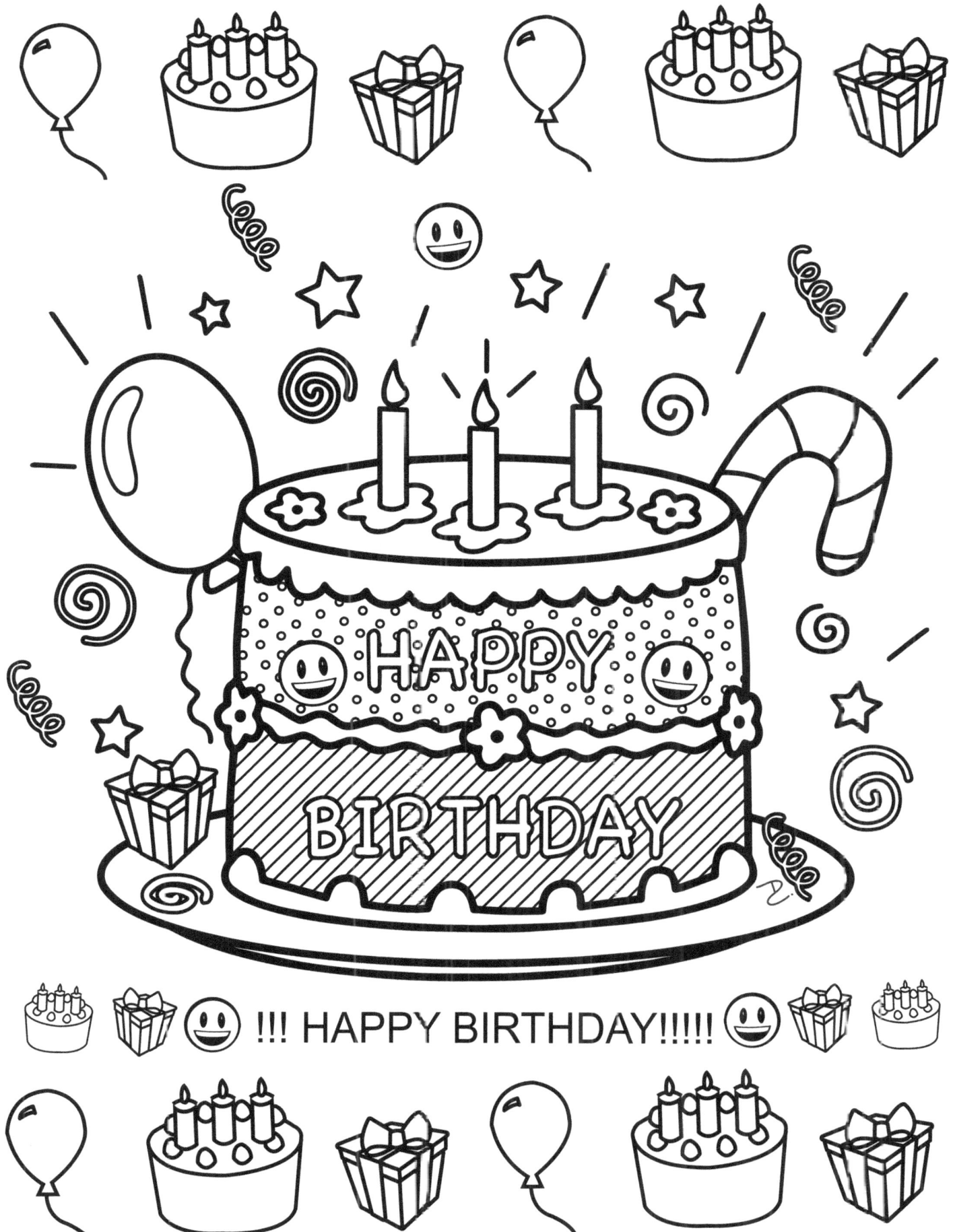

!!! HAPPY BIRTHDAY!!!!!

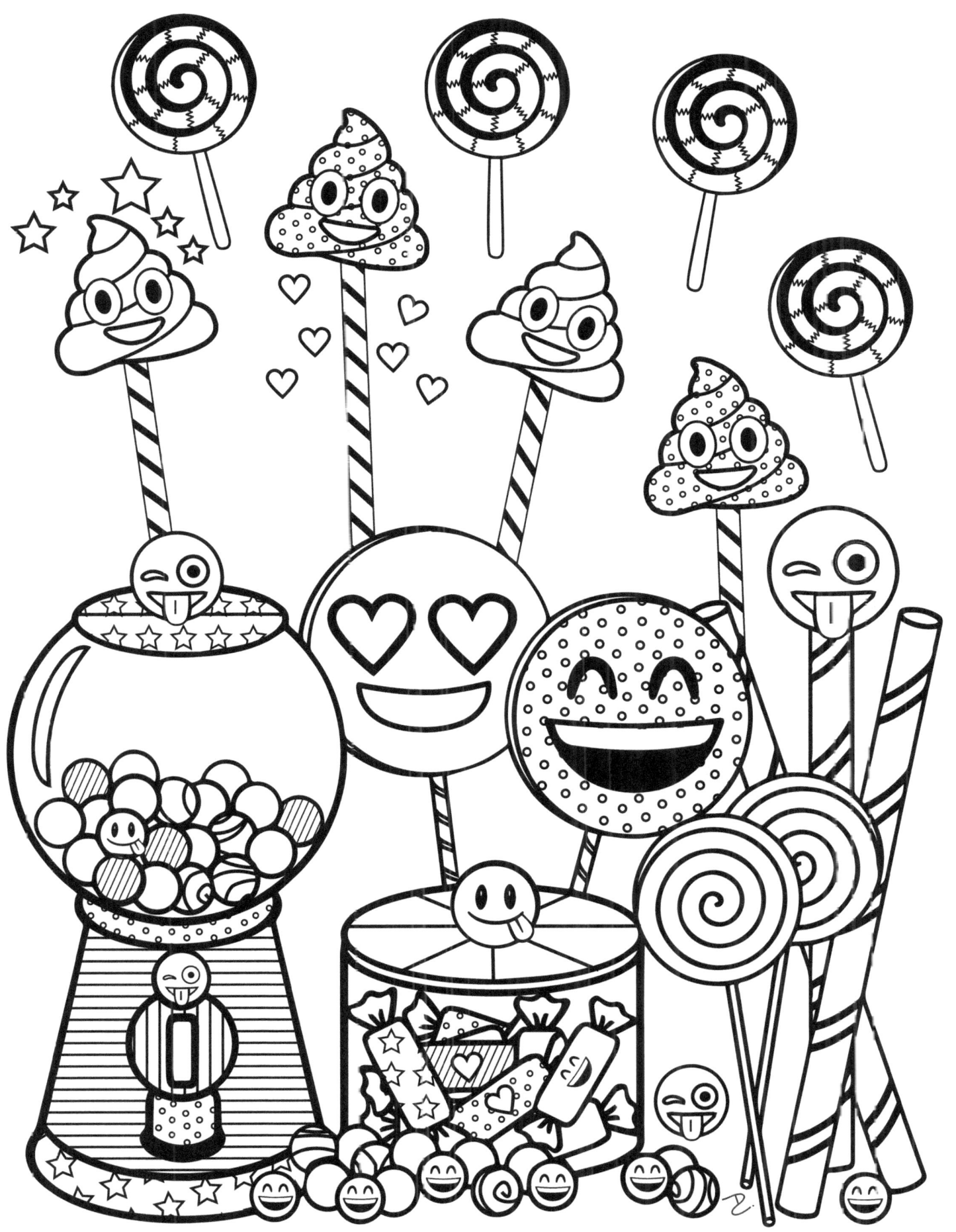

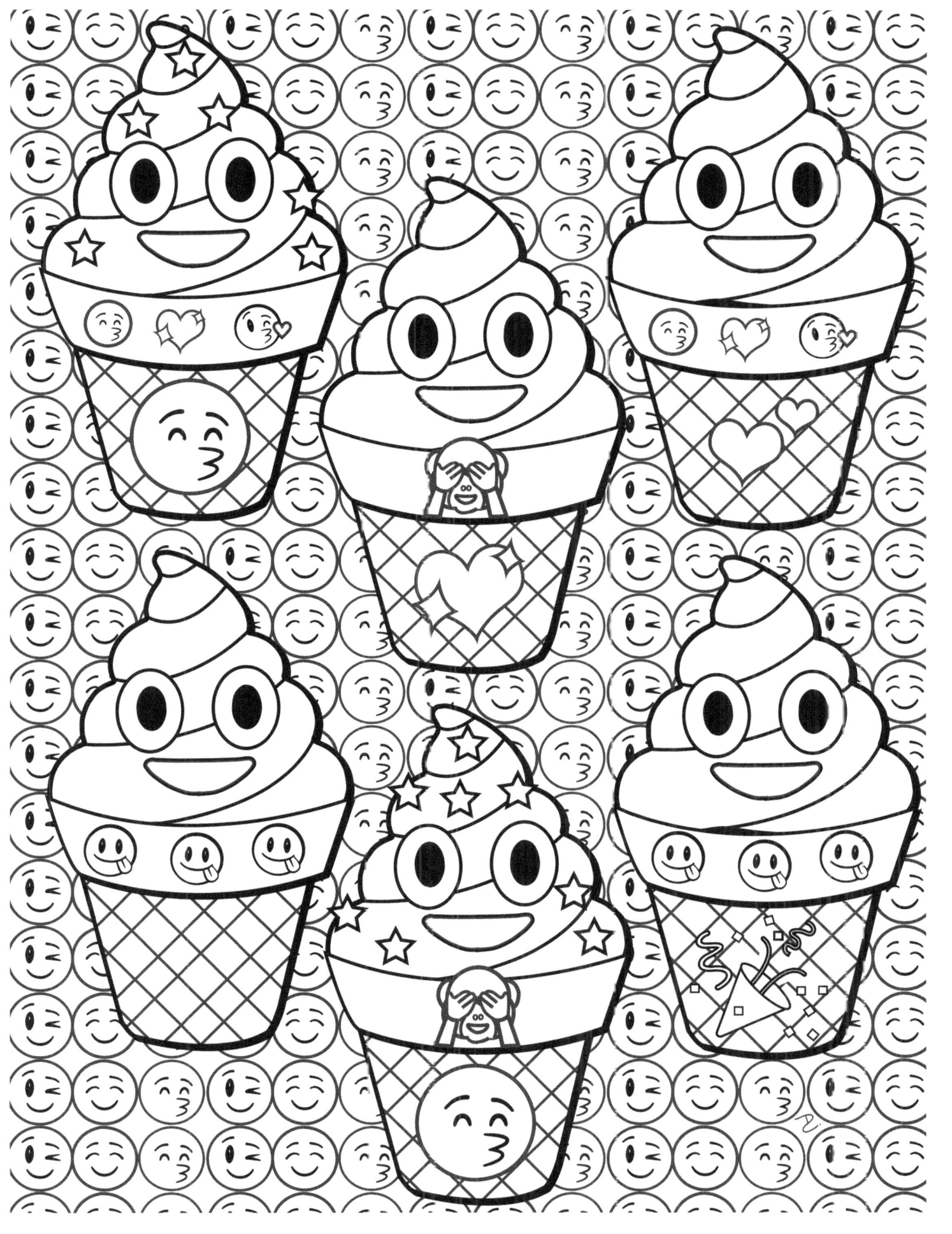